"Animals Have Reason"

"Animals are one of the greatest gifts that life has to offer, we should cherish animals and treat them right, because they deserve to be loved, and so do you."

Written by: Stephanie Ann Hanvey

Dogs are really cute, and they like to play.

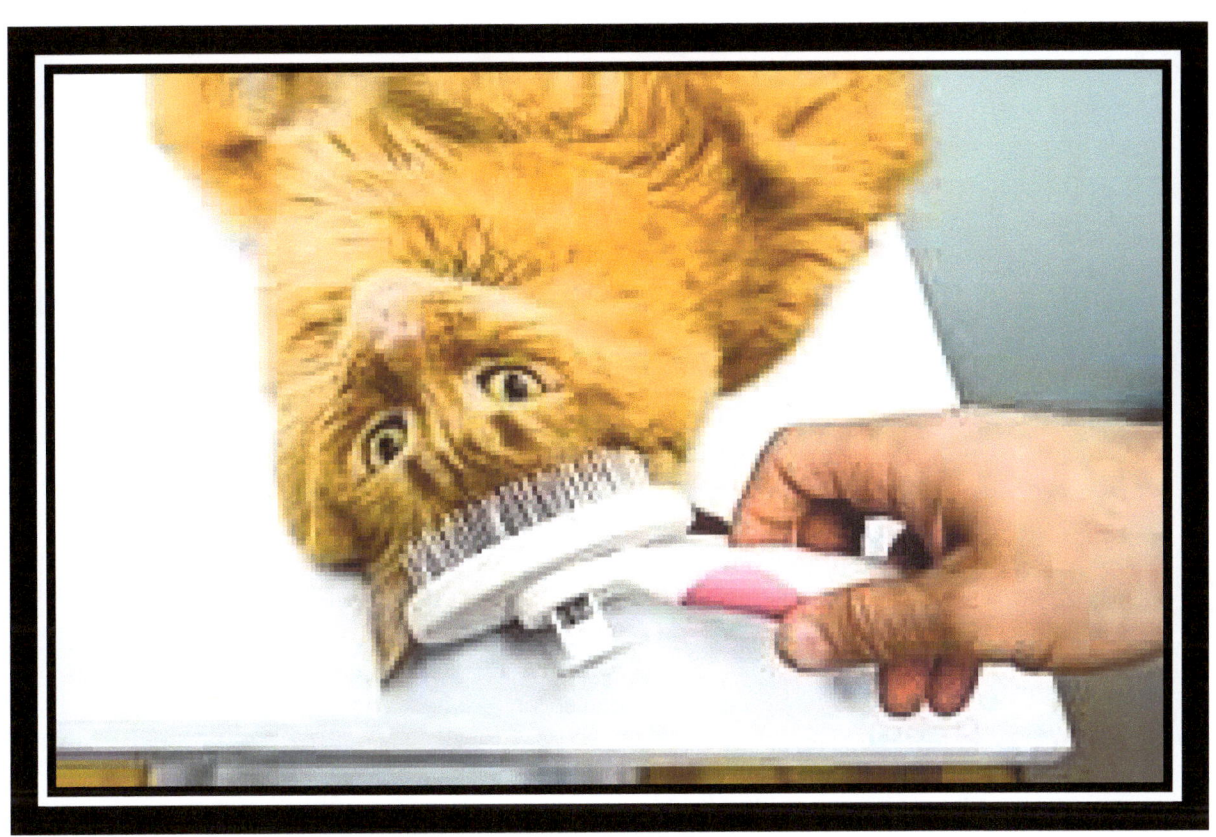

Cats are soft and sweet; make sure to brush them every day.

Hamsters are so nice, and they love to go up
and down their tube.

Snakes are just so neat; I love the way they move.

Birds are amazing, and they like to sing a tune.

Fishes are so pretty; mine like to eat at noon.

Lizards are so cool, and they can swim really well.

Hermit crabs are wonderful; they love to change their shell.

Rabbits are soft and cuddly, and they like to hop, hop, hop.

Turtles are super-slow; but they'll never stop.

Monkeys are the cutest, and sometimes they are wild.

Pigs are so adorable; this one is still a child.

Horses are super-fast, and oh boy can they run.

Dolphins are so awesome; they love to have some fun.

Cows are so sweet, and they like to make us milk.

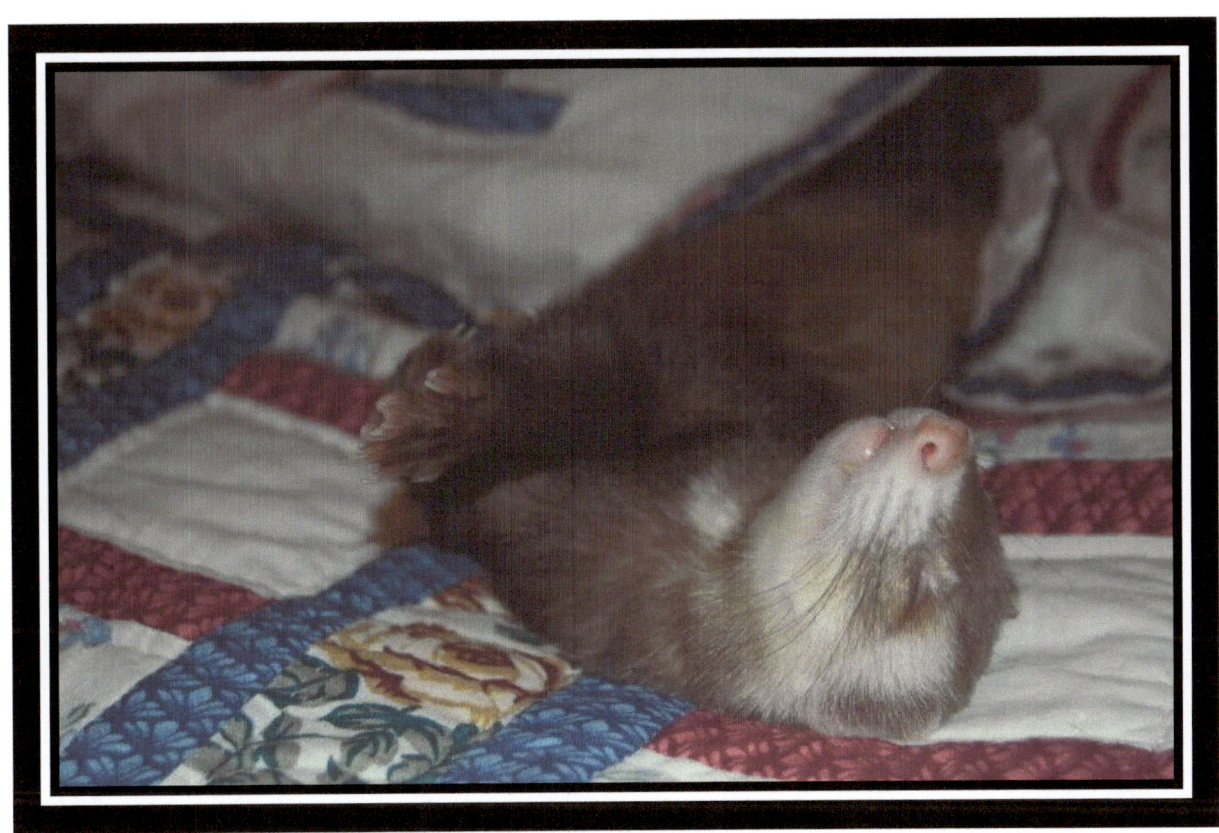

Ferrets are adorable; this one is sound asleep on a quilt.

Frogs are super-neat, and they like to jump
real high.

Polar bears are really cute; but it's time to say goodbye.

The world is filled with so many animals, and
we should love them every day.

It is up to us to care for them, and to make sure that they are ok.

Animals make a difference, because they bring joy to us all.

We should love them no matter what, even if they are small.

So make sure to love your animals, and show them every day, because if you love them very much, they'll always want to stay.

Don't forget to share your love for animals with your family and friends, because if we all love each other, the world will never end.

This is not the end, but the beginning of love.

The End!

Love the world, and love the animals of the world.

Just because we are small,
doesn't mean we dont have reasons.

Help Us
Stop
Animal
Abuse

Animals have a reason, and a purpose, just like
you and me.

We can change the world, if we work together, so join the fight and make a difference. The animals are counting on you!

Special thanks to all the wonderful animals of the world. Thank you for making life extra special!

Remember children! Never forget to love, because love can overcome any obstacle, and if we stick together we can make a positive change in our world.

"A man, who stands alone, is just a lonely man, but a man with many followers is a strong man."

Quote by: Stephanie Ann Hanvey

Use this page to draw your favorite animal.